Anxiety, Anxiety, Why Do You Have a Hold on Me?

Monique Hebert

ISBN-13: 978-1717517593

ISBN-10: 1717517595

To Pa-Pa
my anchor
&
Ge-Ge
my sail

Introduction

As someone who has suffered from anxiety for practically my whole life, I know how incredibly hard it can be. It has challenged me in ways that I could never have imagined, but I wouldn't be me without it.

I was born with anxious tendencies, and my mom would describe me as a very anxious baby. As I went through childhood and eventually my teen years, I became very socially anxious. All that time I still knew nothing about anxiety disorders, but in college I got a rude awakening and realized that something wasn't right. I finally got help my sophomore year and learned I had an anxiety disorder. Since then I have been through many ups and downs, but the thing that has stayed the same and provided me with the most comfort through it all is writing.

Writing has become my favorite form of therapy because it's truly the safest place to let all my emotions out. I have always been the kind of person who can say more through writing than speaking. I know many other people who struggle with anxiety have found writing to be helpful, and I encourage it. Most of these poems I wrote in some of my worst moments. They came from times when I was having a panic attack or full-on meltdown. I write in those moments to help me overcome; it's as if I have this poison in my bloodstream called anxiety, and the only way to release it is by putting pen to paper. My pen is my sword to battle anxiety, and that's why I write.

So why do you write?

I think whether or not you struggle with anxiety, you can relate to the need to write to better yourself and the world around you. That's why I'm sharing these poems. I want people to see they are not alone. So many people fight against anxiety, depression, self-esteem issues, and other mental health problems but never say anything. This is my chance to tell the world yes, I struggle with these things, but that doesn't make me less of a person. It doesn't make you less of a person either; it makes you stronger.

Everyone who has a mental health condition struggles through it differently, but we can all agree that it sucks. We can all relate to dealing with the stigma, having people try to understand (who really can't), and going through the day-to-day struggles of living with a mental health condition. It really does suck, but it hasn't made my life all bad. It's opened my eyes to the world in a different way and has given me a heart to help people just like me. I want to be a light in a world that's full of darkness.

I hope with these poems you can see the insight of an average gal living with her anxiety, but mostly I hope they bring you light on your darkest days and help you see that you're not going through all this alone. There are many people out there, including me, who ask the very same question every day: anxiety, anxiety, why do you have a hold on me?

My Anxiety

I like to think of my anxiety as separate from me, but it isn't. It's a part of me, whether I like that or not, and it took me a long time to realize that. Anxiety has always been in my life and will always remain to some degree. I have learned some amazing coping techniques over the years, but they can never make my anxiety truly disappear. Once I figured that out, I could start to clearly see the good, bad, and ugly side of having an anxiety disorder.

This poem came through learning to accept the way I am and everything that comes with it, including my anxiety. It's hard to accept yourself for exactly who you are because you are always going to have parts of you that you don't like. The best thing you can do is learn to accept those parts of you that make you *you*. Of course I would rather not be anxious, but this is the hand I've been dealt, so I'm going to deal with it the best way that I can. My anxiety has made me do some silly things, but I think of them all as fascinating stories that make life a little crazier but a lot more interesting.

It makes me cry in the bathroom.
It makes me act like a damn fool.
It makes it hard to go on a date,
even harder to celebrate.
It makes me scared to take a chance.
It makes me feel like I'm missing the dance.
It makes it easy to stay alone,
even easier to never leave my home.

It makes me overreact most days.
It makes me walk
through a changing maze.
It makes it hard to tell my friends,
even harder to play pretend.
It makes me wish I could go with the flow.
It makes me mad that I can't say no.
It makes it easy to walk away,
even easier to forget people's names.

When did my anxiety become my identity?
Yes, it's a part of me but it isn't everything.
I'm stronger than I think,
and I'm not always on the brink
of losing a piece of my mind.
I struggle with anxiety, but I'll be fine.

It makes me strong but it makes me weak.
It brings out the best and the worst in me.
It makes me brave but so afraid,

and to be honest I wouldn't change
a thing about me, even my anxiety.

Only Me

Once again I find myself hiding out in a bathroom stall after a panic attack. When I'm out in public and I feel an attack coming on, the bathroom is the first place I go. It becomes my safe space where I try to breathe and bring my anxiety down. Even after the attack is over, sometimes I still stay in the stall out of embarrassment. I don't want to face the world after being the woman who couldn't sit through a movie or walk through a mall or get through a whole class period. In that moment I feel all alone, as though I'm the only one going through this.

But that's not true. There are a million people all over the world in bathroom stalls melting down too. Anxiety is so isolating and makes you feel very alone. Trust me, you are not alone and you will get through this. When you've made it to the other side of a panic attack, you should be proud of yourself instead of beating yourself up. You're only human, after all, and you're not the only one who's been there. We made it through a panic

attack, and so will you, even if it takes
hiding out in a bathroom stall.

Hiding in the bathroom stall
is the woman who thinks she knows it all.
That woman is me and
I'm scared, sitting on my knees,
trying not to make a sound
so nobody will know that I'm around.
This is not where I'm supposed to be,
but this fear has got the best of me.
Now I'm stuck next to this toilet seat.

I got really close to throwing up.
Of course, this is just my luck.
The wave that overwhelmed me
is my own anxiety.
Trying not to be given away
so they will stay far away,
I should be out there making my way
instead of fighting to save this day.
Next to this toilet seat is where I'll stay.

All alone in this stall
as they're pacing down this hall
is sure a strange place to be.
With my head hanging low,
my heart's finally beating slow.

I needed some room to breathe.
Stuff like this happens to only me.

Only me would run away
from the best day of my life.
Only me would stop myself
from being outside.
Only me would give up
the chance to finally get it right.
But I'm the only person
who can give it one more try.

Don't Look Down

This is the first poem I ever wrote about my issues with anxiety. It was written when I was still in college and just learning about social anxiety disorder. I was crippled by fear and anxiety going to class every day, and I had to find a way to get those feelings out, so I wrote about it. It served as a reminder that I could get through the day, even when I felt as if I couldn't make it another minute. I hope it serves as a reminder to you as well: you will get through this if you keep walking and don't look down.

My anxiety has always made me feel like a tightrope walker who's trying to get to the other side but can't. I look down, then lose control and become paralyzed. The only way I will get to the other side is if I keep walking. I know you will have those days when you don't want to keep walking, but you have to, because getting to the other side is so rewarding. When I'm stuck in the middle of the tightrope, I will myself to keep going and keep my head up, because that's all I can do to get by.

When you walk through the door, smile.
Try not to look at the faces.
Don't forget who you are
and how far you've come.
Sit down and take your place.
Remember to keep your head straight.
Love you for who you are,
even the broken parts.
Social anxiety won't get the best
of you today.

When panic runs through your blood,
When fear cripples your soul,
You want to run and hide
from all the people.
When you can't make it through the day
without anxiety stealing your life away,
Have no fear; hope is here
to take you to a better place.
Social anxiety won't get in your way.

Having social anxiety is like
being out on a ledge,
and you're about to walk the tightrope,
but you'd rather fall instead
Because of all the whispers and stares
you see in your head,
making you feel like
you've been left for dead.

When you're walking on that tightrope,
and you can't see the ground.
You start to worry; you start to fear.
But the only thing you have to do is
Don't look down.

Under Control

One of the major things that triggers my anxiety is losing control or not having control over a situation. When that happens, my anxiety creeps up and reminds me with a panic attack that I am not OK. I really hate that feeling. I used to beat myself up over panic attacks, but eventually I realized that getting down on myself never helps the problem. It just makes things worse. Panic attacks come and go; there is no use hiding what you are feeling or being ashamed of it.

This poem is about losing control but also realizing it's OK to not have everything under control all the time. As much as I would love to control every part of my life, I know that's not possible, and understanding that is one of the things that really helped me. The saying "you can't control what happens to you in life, but you can control how you react to it" is so true. I still grapple with getting my anxiety-ridden mind to believe that, but I'm trying every day to react to things in a more positive way.

I told myself it was under control.
I told myself it was manageable.
Now I'm slapped with reality and
my mind's playing tricks on me.
I'll never escape this dream.
It's a recurring theme.

I told myself it wouldn't happen again.
I told myself to be my own best friend.
Now I'm scared of everything and
don't know where to begin.
I guess this is the end.
I'm lost at sea again.

I'm over this feeling.
I'm over the times
when I have to lie and
say everything is fine.
Lying gets easier when
you're trying to reach your goal.
I've got it all under control.

The truth is I have nothing under control.
I'm lying to myself as anxiety takes hold.
I'm over wishing I was someone else,
Someone who takes control.
I just need a little help.

The Elephant in the Room

My therapist tasked me with personifying my anxiety so I could talk about it in a way that felt more real to me. I decided my anxiety is an elephant. I have always liked elephants, because they are big and strong but also very beautiful. My anxiety is just like that. At times it comes stomping in with its big feet, and no one can stop it. No matter where I go, that damn elephant follows me and becomes a literal elephant in the room. Some days the elephant stays calm, and some days it gets mad and takes over. Either way I'm stuck with this elephant for better or worse.

I have a love-hate relationship with that elephant, but at the end of the day it will not go away; I have to deal with it. Pretending that it will go away will not only hurt the problem but make it ten times worse. I hope you can confront whatever animal or person is inside your mind and not pretend the problem will disappear. As tough as that might sound, you need to do it to make real progress.

There's an elephant in the room.
He's sitting next to you.
He follows where I go
and won't leave me alone.
That elephant in the room
makes me want to move.
Where would I go?
Where won't he be known?

That elephant in the room
walked me to my car.
He keeps me on my toes,
and I can't get far
from the elephant in the room.
He took me on a date.
He even showed up late,
but I can't debate.

Don't mind me
and all my insecurities
shaped by my anxiety
that make up
the elephant in the room,
the rock in my shoes,
the curse in my mind,
the madness in my life.
That is all mine.

Me and My Disease

In college I felt like an outcast who didn't get along with anyone or have a purpose. I struggled with being too anxious to speak up in class and had a panic attack nearly every time I walked around campus. I just wanted to be like my classmates whom I perceived as normal. I hated that I struggled with anxiety, and I hated even more that I couldn't talk about it. I kept it bottled in all day.

During one of those sad, frustrating days, I wrote this poem. I felt as if every day I was on a rollercoaster going up and down, but I could never get off. That is the worst feeling in the world, and if you've been there or are there now, then you know how isolating it can be. I wanted to form connections with people, but my disease was always getting in the way.

Now I feel ten times better, because I can talk about my issues not just with my therapist but with my family and friends and even random strangers who are reading this book. It's not worth holding something in when it makes you feel miserable. If you are holding anything in today because of fear of

ridicule or rejection, let it out, because you
will feel ten times better and because you
deserve to live life as you, even if that
means, like me, you tell everyone what an
anxious mess you can be.

I have a good day
that turns to a bad day.
I am happy, then I get sad.
It's like I'm on a roller coaster
with my emotions.
I can't slow down.
I'm just on for the ride.
Can anybody tell me why?

I take medication
to stop the aching,
but then I can't feel.
It's like I'm on a merry-go-round
with my emotions.
I keep spinning to know what's real.
Can you help me feel?

Every day I fight a war and
some days are worse than before.
I never asked for any of this.
I want to go and throw a fit.
Just to be able to feel a little bit.

What's wrong with me?
Why can't I be like normal people?
I want to be set free
from the highs and lows
everywhere I go.
I feel like I'm fighting this alone.
Cause it's just me and my disease.

Depressed

Depression is not a struggle I know very well. Even though there are times when I have felt depressed, I have never been diagnosed with the chemical imbalance of depression. It can be such a tragic disorder, and for most people depression and anxiety go hand in hand. I have known a few people with depression and watched it take over their lives. It makes me sad to think about it. I have also seen them power through their struggle with strength most people never know.

To family and friends of people with depression, first listen to and validate your loved one, even if you can't understand what they are going through. Having a mental health condition isolates you from the world and everyone in it. It feels as if nothing makes sense and you are eternally lost.

If you're lost in this moment, I am there with you, and I'd be ready to run away to another world, but we should stay here. There is more for you and me to do.

She looks in the mirror
and her eyes are still red.

She can't fight the feeling
that it's all in her head.
She lives in the sadness in a big black hole.
She's afraid that the madness
will turn into a sorrow she's never known.
So she wants to go to another world.

She looks out the window
as the world passes by.
Do they even notice that she's dying inside?
She lives in the moment
is something she'd like to say.
But instead she lets time go to waste
and her mind decays.
So she wants to go to another place.

She is lonely; I would know.
She is me and I'm ready to go
to a place in the middle, a place in between,
where depression won't
be able to get to me.

Where I'll live out of the shadows
and I'll be loved by everyone I meet.
I won't live my life in denial.
I will finally be complete.
It's a world that nobody sees,
where my mind doesn't have to be
filled with this mess; not depressed.

Scars

The first time I heard about cutting was from my friend group in high school. It was long before I was officially diagnosed, but I was already dealing with anxiety every day. I couldn't understand why some of my friends had admitted to cutting before; it just sounded like something they wouldn't do. I had no idea the struggles they were going through or how to step up and help them. I didn't know that they were feeling lost, hurt, and alone and cutting themselves was the only way to help the pain. I also didn't know that one day as an adult, I would think about cutting.

When you are stuck in that mind space and you just want the pain to go away, cutting seems like the best option. I've held knives and scissors in my hands multiple times and thought about doing it; that is where this poem comes from. It comes from a place of pain but also from a place of hope, because many people have beaten the urge to cut, and I know you can too. If you need help with this, reach out to people whom you trust, whether that is a friend, teacher, parent, or therapist. Those scars that

are left behind are your battle wounds from
fighting a condition that claims way too
many victims. Don't be ashamed of your
scars, because it's where you've been, but
have hope for the future where you can live
scar free.

I reached for the knife.
It was in plain sight.
I knew what I had to do
to help me pull through.
Just a little cut produces
just a little blood.
I won't feel a thing
until I do it again.

Some people like to
see themselves bleed.
It reminds them that
they're alive.
Some people just
want to die.
They cover up their scars,
but they can't really hide.
Soon they'll miss their chance
to say goodbye.

Scars don't define you.
I know cause I've been there too.
You can cut your pain away,
but the scars will always remain.

It's Not Pretty

When I go out into the world, I put a smile on my face and pretend everything is fine. I even had a coworker tell me once how wonderful it was that I was always smiling. I took it as a compliment but thought, *If you only knew what's going on in my mind* . . . Even some of my closest friends will be shocked to read about my low points in this book. I care so much about what everyone else thinks about me that I can't let them see me hurting. Maybe I'm prideful, or maybe I'm scared that if they saw that side, they would see how ugly it can be.

It's never pretty to witness a breakdown or anxiety attack, and I wish everyone, including me, could get over being self-conscious about it. We all have good and bad days, and we should let people see us at our worst, because if they can't handle you at your worst . . . You know how the rest goes. Life is not pretty. It has beautiful moments, but it's not all roses, and that's OK. Not everything will be picture perfect. Nobody's life is that way, so don't be ashamed that your breakdown is not

wrapped in a pretty little bow; mine never
are either.

Nobody knows how low I've been,
the places I've traveled,
and the things I've hid.
They just see a smile on a pretty face,
but they don't know where
I was yesterday.

Nobody knows about that night.
I cried and almost took my life.
They just see bright eyes
on a beautiful face.
They don't know how deep
I've felt pain.

I've got it all together
from the outside looking in,
but no one sees the part of me
that struggles to live.
The feelings never go away.
The pain comes back every other day.
The breakdowns are like
nothing you've ever seen.
It's not pretty, trust me.

The End of the World

My mind always goes to the worst possible scenario. Even though I'm a pretty positive person, anxiety makes me an extreme worrier. Little things become big things, and before you know it, I'm so overwhelmed that I can't think straight. If you've been there, you know how hard being an overthinker and an overreactor can be. It's the hidden superpower of those with anxiety, and it doesn't go away.

I wish I wasn't hardwired this way, but it's simply who I am and I have to accept it. If I can keep supportive people around me, though, all of these things start to feel less scary. So find some good people to surround yourself with who know you're not being overdramatic—the kind of people who stand by you when you're an anxious mess. I'm fortunate to have people in my life who accept me, anxious mind and all. They help keep me grounded when I'm ready to fly off the handle, and my life is incredibly blessed and a lot more stable because of them.

To me everything's the end of the world.
Everything is worse than before and
I can hardly breathe.
Some nights I lay awake in my bed,
because I can't turn off my head.
Sleep doesn't come easily.

It's true I tend to overanalyze.
I'm the first one to criticize.
I can't brush it all aside.
I wish I was like everyone else
instead of figuring out how to self-help.
It's no good for my health,
but I'll survive.

I'm a triangle in a world of squares.
Sometimes I feel like I'm not really there.
So keep me close and I won't be scared.
The end of the world is coming,
but I'm prepared.

Me Too

Suicide is a scary subject that affects so many, but few are willing to talk about it. It's a dark secret that people who have had suicidal thoughts or have attempted suicide keep hidden. As I heard more people's stories about how they'd been suicidal, I couldn't believe how common it was. So many people have been there; we need to stand by the ones who are feeling it right now and share our stories to educate people.

I've been there too. I was so low that I almost took a whole bottle of pills my freshmen year of college to end it all. Since then I have fought feelings of hopelessness, asking myself why my life matters and if anyone would even notice if I disappeared. When those thoughts creep up, I remind myself that other people have felt the same way. If you are feeling that way now, know that you matter and your life is worth it, even if you don't feel that at all. The world would miss your presence, even if you wouldn't miss it. Don't be ashamed of feeling suicidal. So many people do and have, including me.

Even though I wrote this before the
Me Too movement, I think this poem
testifies to the power of what happens when
we all share our stories. Regardless if that is
sexual assault or suicide or anything else,
when we stand up together and make our
voices heard, we can discover that we are
not in this fight alone.

You're scared; me too.
You think no one cares; I do.
When the only way out is doing
something you'd never thought you'd do,
you're lost; me too.
You think no one will miss you,
but that's not true.
Don't be ashamed of your thoughts,
cause I've been in your shoes.

You've been hurt; me too.
You think you're better off in the dirt;
please don't do
Life is tough, but you're
stronger than you knew.
You want to let go; me too.
Holding on hurts so much;
I tried it too.
Just because you hurt today doesn't mean

you should take yourself out of the game.
You want to erase yourself
from the picture.
You want to end your chapter in this book,
thinking no one knows
what you're going through,
but I do.
When you feel hurt, alone,
angry, scared, confused,
not knowing what to do,
I've been there too.

I wanted it all to end, but trust me,
suicide isn't your friend.
You don't want to hurt any longer,
but that doesn't mean you have to
put it to an end.
It seems too much for you,
but I've been in your shoes.
Raise your hand if you ever
wanted it to be through.
Me too.

The Hardest Person to Love

I always thought when I was a kid that the hardest person to love would be your enemy—someone who had really hurt you in some way. As I got older, I realized that the hardest person for me to love was not my enemy but myself. To be honest, most days I'm not even sure I *like* myself. I can come up with a thousand things about me that I would want to change, and number one would be having an anxiety disorder. That doesn't give me the right to treat myself badly though, because at the end of the day, I am stuck with little ole anxious me; I have to live with that.

I wrote this poem after another long day of beating myself up. I started thinking, *How am I supposed to spread love out into the world if I am not giving any to myself?* It's not selfish to make sure you are taking care of yourself first, because if you don't, how are you ever going to help someone else? Especially if you have a mental health condition, it's important to practice self-care, because love is the enemy of mental illness. Loving yourself may not cure whatever you are battling, but it will sure enough help you

fight it better knowing you are in your own
corner.

I guess I don't love me,
cause I treat me so poorly.
I look out for everybody else
except myself.
I tear myself down.
I push me around.
I need to stop worrying
about everybody else.

My self-esteem must be way low,
even though I try to take the high road.
I need to find out who I am
and learn to say no.
If I could love me,
it would be the boost I need.
Nobody else can love me
the way I could if I could only see.

How can I give love away
when I haven't given any to me?
How can the hardest person to love
be the face staring back at me?

I Stop

If you haven't noticed, I think about myself a lot. Most of the time I'm thinking unpleasant things about me, but it's still always about me. It's damaging to think about only yourself when you have this huge world out there.

This poem came from an experience when I stopped thinking about myself, and it helped my anxiety out a ton. I was having a stressful, anxious, woe-is-me kind of day, so I decided to clear my head with a walk. On my walk I came across a homeless woman whom I saw all the time in my neighborhood. I decided to talk to her and buy her a cup of chili. That one experience opened my eyes so much, because I realized that not everything is about me. I didn't walk away from that experience thinking I was a better person for helping her, but I walked away with the realization that my life isn't so bad. I may have an anxiety disorder and self-esteem issues, but I'm also fortunate enough to be able to go see a therapist and have supportive people around me when others don't. It's not easy walking in my shoes, but I'm sure it's not easy walking in that woman's shoes either.

When I have a day where I'm obsessing over one of my flaws or anxiety-related issues, I tell myself to stop and think about someone else. It may be as simple as calling a friend to ask about their day or talking to a stranger on the bus. When I do that, it makes my problems seem small compared to the rest of the world and gives me a strong dose of much-needed reality.

Five hundred times a day I think about me,
the things I like and the things I need.
I never stop to think
about those beyond my reach.
I complain about my looks.
I complain about my life,
the things I did wrong
and the things I got right.
I never stop to see
those walking in front of me.

In a million different ways,
I'm hurting myself
by looking at my problems
and not someone else.
I never stop to worry if they need my help.

I look in the mirror every single day,
to criticize myself or give me praise.
I never stop to wonder,
Why don't I be the change?

I only see what I want to see.
Only I hurt when only I bleed.
So the focus stays on me,
but I know that I should be
looking out instead of looking in
so I can see where I stop
and the world begins.

Plastic

Let me take you back to a Christmas memory, but let me warn you, it isn't pleasant. It's Christmas Eve, and I'm supposed to be going to church with my family, but I'm super anxious and upset. I don't want to go and sit around jolly, happy people who don't know what I'm going through. I feel as though if I go, I will have to put on a smiling face and be "plastic," and I hate having to fake it through life because I'm feeling miserable. So I decide to go to church as grumpy, anxious me instead of shiny, happy plastic me.

And you know what happened? Everything turned out fine. People could see I was in a bad mood, so they were extra nice to me and tried to be understanding. My worst fear was that people would be upset I wasn't plastic or shiny or happy, but no one was.

I'm scared to show my emotions, because I think people can't handle them. So I tell myself that I have to be plastic at church, school, work, or really anywhere. If you have ever felt plastic, then you know how horrible it feels. It's not being real, and it's not the way to live your life. It's OK to feel whatever you are feeling and to let people in on it. They can handle your emotions, and if they can't, let them go. You are better off without them. Don't let your anxiety make you feel as if you have to hide your true self from the world. You don't deserve to feel like a piece of plastic.

Some days I feel like plastic,
like I'm made of elastic.
I put on my fake smile
and walk through the door.
Some days I stop believing,
because I am still grieving.
I'm still fighting,
but I don't know what it's for.

Some days I look so perfect,
so no one can really see
that it's a struggle to get out the door
and remember how to breathe.
Some days I let the tears out
when no one's around to see.
That way they can never say
I am incomplete.

It's so easy being plastic.
It's so hard being me.
It's better when I don't feel anything,
On that much I agree.
The emotions just get pushed further down.
My feet get planted deep in the ground.
At least this way I'll get what I need.
Being plastic is the only way I'll succeed.

Plastic only lasts so long,
and one day it will all be gone.
So I will have to face the world
as a lonely, sad, and broken girl.
Then they'll get to see the real me.

It's so hard being plastic.
It's much better being me.
It's easier when I feel things,
even if it scares me.
The emotions all start pouring out.
My feet start to move as I open my mouth.
At least this way I can be free.
Being plastic is not the way to be.

Thirteen-Year-Old Me

One day I was thinking about writing a letter to my thirteen-year-old self and wondering what I would say to her. When I thought back on who I was then, I saw that my main mistake was that I really didn't like myself. I thought I was ugly, had bad hair, wasn't popular enough, didn't have enough friends—the list goes on and on. The worst part is that I felt that way well into my twenties. Sometimes when I'm hard on myself today, I still feel like that thirteen-year-old deep down inside. I have to let her go to see the amazing person I am reflected in the mirror.

You have to let go of your thirteen-year-old self or your sixteen-year-old self or your twenty-one-year-old self too. Never forget who you used to be, but grow from that person into someone who can see themselves clearly, flaws and all, and still love themselves. I wish I could have learned this earlier, but at least I learned it at all. It's never too late to show yourself the love you deserve and truly get to know you. If it took me being an awkward, anxious thirteen-

year-old to get here today, then it was totally
worth it.

Thirteen-year-old me didn't like herself.
She wanted to be someone else.
She couldn't see how awesome she was
or the things she would do
or the person she'd become.

Thirteen-year-old me was always alone.
She didn't have many friends
or own a cell phone.
She didn't fit in.
She really stood out.
Now I see that as a good thing
and what life's all about.

Thirteen-year-old me never went on a date.
She hardly talked to boys.
She couldn't quite relate
to people her own age,
but they sure seemed great.

Thirteen-year-old me told herself lies,
that she was ugly
and would never get a guy.
She believed those lies
almost her whole life.

If I could go back in time,
I'd get myself back in line.
I'd look at me a different way.
I would no longer be ashamed
of what I see when I look at me.
That's what I'd go back and teach
thirteen-year-old me

Slipped

Along with going through the ups and downs of having an anxiety disorder, I also struggle with my self-esteem. My lack of self-esteem seems to come from being constantly overwhelmed by anxiety that I can't control. As I went through counseling working on both, I would often beat myself up after setbacks in my progression toward a healthier life. When I would have another panic attack or my anxiety would hold me back from achieving something, that mean voice in my head would overreact and make me feel bad about myself.

During one session my awesome therapist told me that when you're climbing the staircase of life, you aren't always falling all the way down to the bottom. Sometimes when you have setbacks, you just slip on a stair instead of falling, and you should treat yourself better. That small piece of advice clicked in my brain, and I wrote this poem to inspire me and those around me to be nicer to yourself as you embark on this daily war with anxiety. Everyone has setbacks; please don't beat yourself up over them. Your self-worth is not tied to what

you are doing in life, who you are dating, or
what job you have, and it most certainly is
not tied to battling a mental health condition.
Learning to treat myself better has helped
improve my anxiety, which has in turn
assisted me in loving myself for who I really
am.

You're so hard on yourself.
Your downright mean.
You say you're a failure
and there's no in-between.
I know the truth that you can't see.
You're going to be OK,
so just listen to me.

The things you say to yourself
are incredibly rude.
When you talk that way, you're sure to
lose.
I know one day you will finally see.
You're amazing as you are;
you just need to believe.

When you're climbing a ladder
or you're going up stairs,
I know you get nervous feeling unprepared.
You might have had a setback
when you thought you were standing tall,

but at least you can say
that you give it your all.
You only slipped, you didn't fall.

You can be your own worst enemy
or your own best friend.
You'll make mistakes sometimes,
but this isn't the end.
You can get back up every time you fall.
This time you didn't go
all the way to the bottom.
You just slipped, you didn't fall.

Some Stories Are Meant to Be Told

I used to think I had nothing interesting to say. I'm a rather quiet person, so I thought, *Why would anyone ever listen to me or take me seriously?* Anxiety crept in and made me feel worthless—until I found my voice and realized I had a story to tell. My story may not sound like your story, and yours probably won't look like mine, but isn't that the beauty of us all being so different? We each have a unique story, and it's our right to tell it. Never let anyone tell you that your story isn't valid or worth telling.

For years I let my anxiety keep me down with my mouth shut. Now I'm telling the world who I am and what I've been through. That's what this poem is all about, being brave enough to tell your story. All of these poems are the story of my life so far that I want to share with you. I'm being brave so you can be brave enough to tell your story proudly. My life has changed from hearing people tell who they are, where they came from, and how they got to where they are today. You can change the world

just by being you. I've shared my story; now
it's your turn.
What's your story?

The story of your life begins every day
when you decide to wake up and
live a certain way.
It takes you through the good.
It takes you through the bad.
All the moments you're happy and
the ones when you're sad.

The end of one story
always starts another one.
Sometimes it feels like magic
when the day is done.
It takes you through the rainbow.
It takes you through the rain.
The memories that make you smile
and the ones that leave you pain.

Some books are meant to be opened
before it's too late.
Some chances are worth taking
and some are left up to fate.
It matters how you live
so learn to forgive before you get old.
Some stories are meant to be told.

You'll always have a choice.
You'll always have a chance
to tell your story
no matter the circumstance.
So tell it proud.
It doesn't matter what they say.
You might not fit the mold
but some stories are meant to be told.

Until My Fingers Bleed

Writing has saved me. It has helped me deal with anxiety, panic attacks, low self-esteem, and suicidal thoughts. Not everyone can relate to that, and writing may not be your form of therapy, but I encourage you to find something that helps you balance out your mental health and to pursue whatever that is. If I couldn't write, I don't know where I would be. Through the written word I'm able to express everything I want to say but often can't.

If you've read these words and poems, then you've seen a clearer, truer me than what I portray to the world. I've never been able to talk about my anxiety out loud, but give me a paper and pen and you'll hear it all. That is the beauty of what writing can do, and I hope it does that for you. You don't have to write to please anyone else; do it for you. No one even has to see what you write, but putting your feelings down on paper can feel so good. I don't claim to be an expert writer, but without it I wouldn't be me, and honestly, I don't think I'd survive.

I need to put words on a page
to remind me of my better days.
I need to write what I can't say,
or this feeling will go away.

The pages bleed from my soul
to say the things I feel inside.
This pen will be wrapped around my finger
until the day I die.

The singer has a song,
and the writer has a page.
So I'm going to use my words
in the best possible way.

My fingers will go numb,
but my mind will roam free.
When I put words on a page,
it fills the empty space inside of me.

All I need is paper and a pen,
then I can tell my story to the end.
It's not easy to write about your life,
but it's the therapy I need tonight.
So I'll write everything I see
until my fingers bleed.

Makes You Strong

You want to know what I think strength is? Strength is my mother, who will do anything to help her family. Strength is also my brother, who went to a war zone at twenty-one and made it out alive. Strength is you, who gave this book a chance and read it all the way to the end. Most importantly, I think strength is when you just keep going on.

Life is hard; life with a mental health condition is even harder. It breaks you, and most days you don't want to go on, but you do. Most days I don't want to get up and deal with my anxious mind, but I do. I have to reassure myself every day that the strongest thing I can do is keep fighting the good fight and not give up. Everyone has moments when they are ready to give up, but that doesn't define you. I am not defined by the times I wanted to drop out of college or stop writing this book. I kept going and graduated from college, and more impressively, I put all my jumbled thoughts to paper and wrote this. I know there are many things I haven't been successful at and won't be in the future, but I keep going.

Even when my anxiety tells me to stop and
backs me into a corner, I keep going. I have
to and so do you.
Keep going. It might just save your life.

You want to know what strength is?
It's rocking the boat when everyone
told you to give up hope.
It's the quiet voice that says
you'll be OK after the end of a long day.

You want to know what breaks you
each and every day?
It's thinking your strength
can be given away.
You'll never know how strong you can be
until you've had to face defeat.

It's in the way you don't give up.
It's in the way you act so tough
when the fact of the matter is
you're afraid to try again.
You've got your whole life long,
and that's what makes you strong.

Do you really want to know
what makes you strong?
It's your ability to keep holding on.
Do you really not see

that you've been strong all along?
You get up each day
and fight when things go wrong,
and that's what truly makes you strong.

Conclusion

I hope this book has made you more optimistic about your own struggle with anxiety. I also hope that, through reading my story and these poems, you've been able to laugh and cry along with me on this anxious road we're navigating. Even though this book can't give you all the answers for how to break the hold anxiety has on your life, know that someone else is out there struggling too. You are not in this battle alone, and as we each share our stories, I know we will help break the stigma around mental health conditions and anxiety together.

So keep writing and keep loving yourself, because you deserve to be shown some love. On your bad days and good days, hold your head up high and take a deep breath, because you've got this. Anxiety may be a part of you, but it's not your whole story. Always remember that.

Anxiety, anxiety, why do you
have a hold on me?
You might have held me back yesterday,
but you will not win this war today.

Acknowledgements

I would like to thank: Kirstin Andrews for editing this book and encouraging me along the way. My mother, Marie for being my biggest fan and shoulder to cry on. My aunt, Carla for listening to me rant about writing, theatre, and everything in between. My grandparents, Thelma (Ge-Ge) and Ferdinand (Pa-Pa) who are no longer with us, but are smiling down on me. To every therapist I ever had who has seen me at my worst and celebrated with me at my best. I can't forget about every English teacher I had in school for instilling a love of reading and writing in me. To every church community I have been a part of: thank you for showing God's love to me in my darkest moments. A huge thank you to everyone who picked up this book and gave it a chance. I appreciate you more than you know.

About The Author

Monique Hebert is a writer who is originally from Cleveland, Ohio but now resides in Seattle, Washington. She graduated with an English degree from Cleveland State University in 2014. She loves writing the three P's; poems, personal essays, and plays. She has written for *The Mighty*, *Living Lutheran*, and *Broadway World*. When Monique's not writing you can find her reading a self-help book, laughing with family, advocating for mental health in her community, or going to see a theatrical production.